AF482013

Table of Contents

Dedication

This collection is dedicated to Eric Luthi, Sian Martin, and Ruchi Acharya, all editors who believed in my poetry very early on.

Acknowledgments

Here on this page, I would like to express and list my sincere appreciation for my journey as a poet and as I enter deeper into the literary world. Though a relatively new traveler in this world of words, I have been able to accomplish some considerable success with the help and support of many people. Firstly, I have to thank my family for their support and faith in me, for them having to read poetry even though they don't particularly like poetry. Especially my wife, Diane, whether she liked some of the poems or not, she read most of them.

Most importantly in the literary realm, I must thank the editor of Underwood Press, Mr. Eric Luthi, who saw something in my work early on and published me for the first time. I also owe him a lot for the guidance and the education I got from working with him, as he has published my work several times now and invited me to be a reviewer for Underwood. This has been an invaluable experience for me that has led to other opportunities for publication in other journals, magazines, and anthologies thus far. *(see publication history on page 90)*

There were other reviewers and editors along the way with other publications that offered advice and counseling, whether they published my work or not. One such editor I must mention and acknowledge by name is Sian Martin, poetry Editor-in-Chief for Tempered Runes Press. Her very insightful critique of five of my poems gave me some new perspectives and ideas on how I could improve my craft. Special thanks to Ruchi Acharya, Editor-in-Chief of Wingless Dreamer Publishers for her words of encouragement and appreciation for my work.

Lastly, but certainly not in the least, I would like to thank my fans. Yes, I do have some that I know of, and hopefully, they are growing in number. The big payoff for me is when someone can relate to and enjoy one of my poems. That reward is called gratification, then I feel I've accomplished my goal, I've done my job. I don't write just for me, though it is my joy, I also write for the readers and hopefully their satisfaction.

Introduction

From the feedback that I have received from editors and publishers and from doing research, it seems the consensus is, that a chapbook or full-length book of poetry should have a theme and that the poems should have continuity, connected to each other in some fashion. I am a poet of diverse styles, forms, subjects, and genres. My body of work varies greatly, as I like it to be. Just one style, one form, or genre would be very confining and boring for me. However, for this book, I have attempted to focus on my poems with one thing in common, they are poems that are comments on different life scenarios, situations, and observations on topics that are either tied to times from yesterday, or today, but always applicable to now as in these times, and probably will be tomorrow. I hope you enjoy this collection of some of my work.

Poem No. 1
Walking on Ice, Recalled

Have you ever climbed a glacier's face?
  Have you ever went walking on top of a mountain of ice?
  …You know, way up north someplace.
Standing high above the valley and the glacier stream below,
I took in a wonderous scenery not many will ever know,
upon the Eklutna Glacier all covered with snow.
  The sun was out shining so bright with its reflection,
  no other soul is in sight, I savored the complete isolation.
With a bit of a chill down my spine when I would tentatively pass,
the expanse and great depth of each and every crevasse.
  With every step carefully chosen,
  I walked on that silent body of water for millennia frozen.
If ever given the chance I wouldn't think twice,
for the thrill of walking again, on that kind of ice.
  Knowing that should I see all this melting on some future day,
  the world will be hurting and paying a terrible price.
I'm hoping for the best scenario some way,
so in my future days, I can again walk upon this ice,
hoping for somehow, it will continue to stay.

Now 50 years later, in some current pictures I see,
my hope seems to have been sadly in vain.
  For I can gauge the change over that span that's so apparent to me.
The mouth of the great glacier is much wider now, it's so plain,
much further back into the gorge than it used to be.
  The ice where I walked is long gone now just a memory, now just empty air.
My advice, if you'd like to go walking on ice, better hurry up and get up there.

Poem No. 2
Waterfall

Water racing over the edge with no hesitation at all,
unable to resist that gravity's call.
Unwavering in that downward direction we see it pull.
Waterfall.
Like a waterfall,
        life can go crashing down with great speed,
       while we're just trying to fulfill a need.
        Sitting safely above the ledge, survival indeed.
         Nothing ventured nothing gained, as the saying goes.
         While everyone knows,
           it can be scary as Hell,
            looking over that ledge and letting go.
            But we know all too well,
            in order to prosper and grow,
             sooner or later, we need to go with the flow.
            We can't stay upstream forever.
            Though it may be comfortable to,
             in our hearts, we know what we need to do.
            If we stood still then we'd never know,
            what wonderful possibilities our lives might show.
            It could be the best thing ever,
             ....what's waiting here below!

Poem No. 3

Shelter

Whether of sticks or stones,
 a place to warm the bones.
  Shelter, a safe place to wait out the storms,
  when the lightning and thunder forms.
A cave can be or a mansion by the sea,
 it really doesn't matter, either one can be.
  A dry space for when the rain comes,
   something to hold in the heat from the cold that numbs.
Shelter, a break from the wind when it wails,
a shield strong against the gusts until the wind curtails.

A shelter can be a fortress or a shack,
  if you want your shelter to be a home though,
  here is what you may lack,
   someone there to share it with, some companionship to know.
That itself a shelter against loneliness,
a kind of shelter may be more needed, and more precious.
  A shelter built by love and trust in each other,
   standing strong against life's storms that will not falter.
My wish is for everyone to have a home, and that kind of shelter.

Poem No. 4
It's All About the Pain

It's all right if nature has its rain,
but nobody wants to get wet,
it's way too much of a pain.

A lot of people are trying hard to use their brain,
but it takes a lot of concentration and focus,
for some, it can cause way too much pain.

There are some who should refrain,
telling terrible tales and horrible lies.
It doesn't seem to matter that others will feel the pain.

It's now too much trouble working for what you might gain,
when you have to play by the rules,
it can cause one hassles and causes way too much pain.

Why not cheat to get ahead, and try to catch that "gravy train",
it can be so much easier,
and without causing way too much pain.

All the suffering, it's hard to explain,
some, it seems, care to do nothing righteous anymore,
it might cause them some effort, and way too much pain.

Though these days it would appear, chaos will reign,
while some will speak of love and peace,
they talk of everyone coming together again.
I don't see it happening, too many people will abstain,
they can't open their eyes and their mind,
admitting their part of the problem,
and the cause of, way too much of the pain.

Poem No. 5

Inspiration at an Exterior Coastal Scene

Rocks so rugged and rough,
with edges sharp that would cut a body.
  Sharp enough,
  surfaces unyielding to my flesh,
  they were more than hard enough.
Ah, I breathe in the ocean air...so fresh.
  To my left an outcrop of some sort of oak tree,
  of some short scrubby kind.
Standing like little silent sentinels overlooking the sea.
  Their presence there somehow gave to me,
  a peace of mind.
Barren rocks with no life and so cold.
  The trees show how life can be so bold.
I stand there among them in the battering wind and salty air,
I come to know a new resolution as I reflect on what I see there.
  And on that rocky and desolate shore,
  I realized now more than ever before,
In life one may be faced with adverse conditions and the struggle can be
long.
  In spite of all the things that's hard in life you can overcome it if you
can be strong.
Among the harshest environments life can still flourish and exist.
  So, no matter what you have to live with, you can survive, just persist.

Now as I find a scarce plot of sand,
I watch the ocean waves with such force as it comes and batters the land.
  Relentless assaults, through eons the water has carved this bay.
Nature has made its mark and the ocean has had its way.
  Beneath the cerulean blue sky,
  I ponder many questions that start with why.
Some self-examination asking myself why I should be,
how I should be, why I thought life might be too hard for me.
I just have to be committed to being someone who tries.

(continued on next page)

I realize as I watch the waves build and rise,
I can be a stronger person, that I have it in me to be.
I must acknowledge the effect of this abstract view.
My senses awakened, my mind re-energized, my emotions keen,
feeling fortunate I found my motivation in the solitude of this coastal
scene.

Poem No. 6
Carbon Catastrophe?

Complex molecules in suspension.

                    Multi-chemical composition.

With an elemental basis for it all.

                    Roll it all up in a ball.

Insert a guiding code,

          inject the energy required,

Connected to the correct node.

                    From some superior Creator inspired,

from the primordial soup it strode.

Upon some giant rock in space,

              with all the perils of existence to face.

Standing upright after thousands of centuries,

           standing there on some shore with eyes to see.

After crawling out of the tepid sea,

          developing and displaying great ability,

with a mind to think of what might be,

              a brain to explore every possibility.

The collection, the composite of carbon,

          with other essential elements combined.

A complex creature based on carbon,

          one so unique from somewhere from beyond,

now with a destiny intricately entwined.

          What actions and events will eventually unfold?

And what kind of story will be told?

              What kind of legacy will be spun?

For now, the story has just begun.

(continued on next page)

How far has the creature come,
to what degree is it a success?
Is there reason to believe there's progress?
Is there hope at all for this creature called human,
and for all humanity?
Or are we just one big carbon catastrophe?

Poem No. 7
The Cosmic Machine

The wheels are turning,
the gears are grinding.
   Around and around the whole damn thing goes.
Why it does there's not one single person who knows.
   But the Cosmic Machine just goes, goes, goes.

The entire universe and then some.
   Different dimensions, where did they come from?
Exotic energy flows,
it's the engine and the fuel and it never slows.
   The Cosmic Machine both sucks and blows.

Complete chaos from an outside view,
chaos bound by order, yet there's no boundaries to what it can do.
   From deep within where's there's no end,
   an intelligent design outward to send.
The Cosmic Machine, its existence for eternity we hope will extend.

This much we know, we exist because it does.
   At the very heart of it all lies the result and the cause.
From itself it spewed forth all of creation,
a Prime Element directing each and every evolution.
   A Caretaker to the Cosmic Machine and its operation.

While being such an insignificant speck in the whole damn thing I guess,
doesn't mean for such things I don't have the adequate mind to address.
   After analyzing that which is known, speculating on what is not,
   applying some logic and some old fashion common sense some may
have forgot,
   deductions made producing conclusions so many for so long have
sought.
(continued on next page)

I reflect, I have always wondered why.

A lot of thought, a lot of inner searching as the years went by.
After trying to conform to just one story, a universal explanation,
there always seemed to be missing something from the equation.

Something called the Cosmic Machine by Intelligent Design, the latest
sensation.

Poem No. 8
Believe What You Want

Some may believe in the boogie man,
ghosts, and other spirits that haunt.
  Maybe you don't believe in Santa Claus,
  or the Easter Bunny anymore, and with good cause.
Some people don't know what to believe,
if you ask them to name something, they can't.
  For others, I suppose they don't have to believe in a thing,
  if they don't want.

  Believe in some God or not, it's up to you,
  you can believe what you want,
  but how do you know that it's true?
Maybe believe in a religion others have now forgot.
  Others may believe in fantasies with their illusions,
  oh, how they may taunt.
Some must believe in something,
seeking answers, they have sought.
  Many are left with questioning minds,
  and souls that are left empty and gaunt.

Millions of people tune in every day listening,
to what people on the networks have to say.
  Believing all the talking heads, they can put on quite a show,
  you must know,
  they totally plan it that way.
They tell everyone they're only looking out for you,
that everything they tell you, you must believe is true.
  Do you want to believe in fairytales too?

Believe in your politicians and the leaders of your land,
if that's what you want to do,
but I wouldn't advise you to.

(continued on next page)

Seems every time they go to speak it's just to grandstand.
They tell everyone they're fighting for them,

you can listen to them rant.
  But it's the same old tired message again and again.
But you, of course, can believe what you want.

I believe that if you want to believe in something that can be real,
believe in yourself, that's where to begin, start there first.
  I would hope that everybody has it within them to search, find, and
feel,
  all the great wonder that lies in knowing what our spirits need to
quench the thirst.
A longing desire to know what our lives, life itself, and what it all might
mean.
  With our inner wonderings of how we fit into the overall plan,
    so many options, some extreme,
    I believe, a lot of us believe in something in between.

Poem No. 9

Dead Horse Fantasy

There the poor pitiful thing lies,
  A lifeless corpse, drawing flies.
It's been laying for so long there,
  No longer feeling, no longer breathing air.
But despite this pitiful state,
  There's a bunch of idiots that think it's not too late,
They are committed to ride it inspite it's deceased state.
  They continue with great fervor to strike and beat,
In this created fantasy of theirs of course.
  They cannot give up on a bad idea and accept defeat,
Some people call it a "Dead Horse".
  We hear their cries, their screams, and their curses,
As they beat upon their imaginary horses.
  And after so many tries,
Still that dead horse will not rise.
  (some will realize)
But some will continue to beat on,
  Beating with all they have until the hide is gone.
When they beat through the meat and get to the bone,
  They won't leave the dead horse alone.
Still, some may want to keep beating away-
  Even in the horse's sorry state of decay,
But hopefully, soon they won't be able,
  Too exhausted from beating it all day.
Maybe to finally give up their dead-end fable,
  Waking up to reality,
That DEAD is what their horse will stay,
  No matter how hard they don't want it to be.

Poem No. 10
"Bubbles"

It seems like almost every other day,
on the network news or some talk show,
I hear some of the people on there say,
(They're supposed to know)
"People in New York City,
  people down in Washington D. C.,
  and those celebrities out in L. A.,
  all live in "bubbles" out of touch with reality".

I suppose we all live in our own little bubbles of a kind,
little personal bubbles are what comes to my mind.
  Mine is inhabited by family and friends,
  that's pretty much the extent, and where my bubble ends.
But bubbles be they what they may,
I can't hide in mine from the real world I deal with every day,
my life won't afford me that luxury.
  I must accept it; it's going to be what it's going to be.

Some folks who are rich and famous, a celebrity, a star,
powerful politicians, big businessmen, leaders from afar,
their bubbles much bigger and better, a strong refuge from reality.
  They have the option to do what they want, secure in whatever their
fantasy.
Never do they need to worry one bit about the cost,
they always have the money it seems to cover what's lost.
  Those people in bubbles on the east coast, and the coast on the west,
  keep trying to convince me in Arizona, that for me they know best.

Without a single clue,
of what it is that I do,
  Some seem to think they know better.
Why? Because with some paper degrees I suppose,
they think they're a hell of a lot smarter?
(continued on next page)

I don't give a hoot what anyone thinks he knows.
I just want them to stay in their bubble, … leaving me alone,
happy, in a little bubble of my own.

I don't care about theirs,
as long as their bubble doesn't burst mine,
they can keep their insecurities, hang-ups, stresses, and paranoid fears.
I'll be happy and content as far as I'm concerned, I'll be just fine.
   I think those people are crazy, insane, but I don't care what they do.
It's hard to believe the stupid stuff they want us all to go through,
knowledge, intelligence, and common sense are totally different things,
and if the truth hurts, I'm not sorry if it stings.

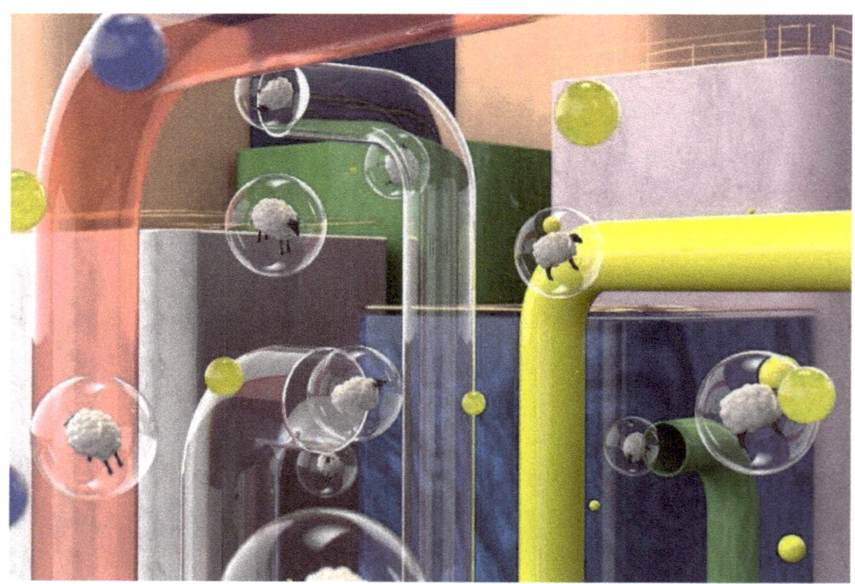

Poem No. 11

Beehives, Ant Hills, and New York City

Watch them scurry about,
across the ground ants to their ant hills they swarm,
working their way in and working their way out.
  Bees busy in their hives hanging in the trees, trying to do no harm.
People, altogether, up and down the streets,
there's no time to stop for acknowledgements and greets.
  All busy, busy with business they toil to do,
  there's always something more important than the individual you.
Into and out of and throughout their structures,
the masses pass, just indiscriminate blurs,
with purpose, …without.
  Trekking on to some ultimate destiny,
  something they probably don't know anything about.
Just treading water or merely marking time for all eternity.
  I wonder why we need a hive, a colony, or a village,
  I see very few reasons I'd want to live like that.
But, hordes of entities swarm together to feast and pillage,
to get what they can from their existence and that's where they gather
at.
  So close their proximity to each other, tightly squeezed together.
In their limited spaces they seldom bother to get to know each other.
  If a Superior being was watching from above,
  evaluating all the species here on this earth,
  could they see any real differences in the basic behavior of?
Any appreciable and actual elements of worth,
between one or the other?
  The differences may be hard to see.
The possible conclusions could quite likely be,
these inhabiting creatures compete,
they kill and eat each other because they like the taste of meat.
  It seems survival of the fittest is the only real rule,
  it doesn't really seem to matter that their existence is so cruel.

(continued on next page)

Every solar cycle sees it all,
nothing much seems to really change day after day, year after year,
as each society continues to dissipate, fade, and fall.
  Lessons that should have been learned a long time ago,
  lacking some ability to retain the knowledge they once came to know.
Observe and catalog the beehives, the ant hills, and New York City,
meccas for certain inhabitants to congregate to do what they do.
  It's a shame, it's a pity, and it's not all that pretty,
  the similarities of these and others are more than just a few.
One would think we could have done better, evolving much more.
  Not to is fine, for beehives and ant hills, but not our cities,
  not for the inhabitants of these,
  but, I guess ,
  we have made some progress,
…we're no longer living in trees.

Poem No. 12
Behind Closed Doors

Dirty deeds done behind closed doors,
  by those who plan, scheme, and conspire to cheat,
  incorporating leakers, liars, and celebrity whores.
Always for their own gain, for the power they must eat,
  only for your support and money do they compete.
Damn these traitorous plots prepared behind closed doors.
Honesty, truth, justice, and any compassion, tossed to the wind,
  the laws and rules to bend,
  no such things at all, not for them.
They will tell you they defend the oppressed,
when really, they only want the means to oppress,
… I'm not impressed!

It's a secret, they don't want to tell anyone.
If the real truth should get out,
  the movement would certainly be over and done.
But they can only speak openly of what it's really about,
  when they're behind those closed doors.
  (And they're not too keen on giving tours.)
There they can discuss whatever it takes,
  whatever it takes, by any means,
  lies, deceit, and stories that are fakes.
These shadow people behind the scenes,
  to achieve their goals and dreams as their anthem roars,
  their diabolical doctrine hatches behind closed doors.

WARNING: Beware of those
 Who try to pose,
  as something they are not.
 Those who meet behind closed doors,
  and what evil they concoct,
  in their star chambers in secret, they plot.

(continued on next page)

When it's expedient for them, if they need a war, they'll start one.
It matters not how many dead bodies there are when they're done.
The bottom line is the bottom line,
  motivated by the almighty dollar sign.
Powered by their billions,
  it's control over people by the hundreds of millions,
  it's the power they have always sought.
May it never be taken for granted or forgot.
You can call it all unfounded conspiracies,
  just wild flights of fancy, some misconceived theories.
But just maybe…what if they're not?

(Give that some thought.)

Poem No. 13
But It Wasn't Up to Me

I was a witness, I was there.
  It was a real pity all the way around.
Someone screamed for help from someone,
somewhere.
  Everyone there was watching it unfold,
  standing like statues so stone cold.
Anyone could have stepped in and stopped it,
no one did, now we may only look back to regret it.
  It didn't have to be,
  but it wasn't up to me.
Like everyone else, I stood still.
  The courage nobody could seem to find.
Or was it more a matter of will,
or an un-willingness to get involved?
  Maybe our consciences have merely dissolved.
(I know I should have done something.)
  Was I the only one with this thought?
Still, no one would do anything,
it's like the concept of compassion had been forgot.
  I saw the whole thing, so unjust,
  we can no longer, in God put our sacred trust.
I should have tried to bring the conflict to an end,
I didn't think it was my place,
  I didn't know anyone there; I didn't see a friend.
I sure didn't want to be the one to face,
all that chaos and dangers that might be.
  I could have been the hero of the day,
  but it wasn't up to me,
Such a shame, that was what everybody had to say.
  With another victim hurt and bloody.
It's now over, as the crowd walks away,
cold and heartless, not seeming to care.
  Is this the kind of life I want to share?
Is this the way I want this life to be?
  I guess it really is up to me.

Poem No. 14

Hard Times

Hard times, people are starting to see hard times.
  They're starting to see just how hard, hard times can be.
I have written of such times,
in poems written out in rhymes.
  Writing of times of mine throughout my days,
  the things I've known and learned in my time, back a ways.
Things I discovered and determined, I've tried to convey,
some messages to folks I've tried to relay.

Hard times like in the past,
now again have become the new reality.
  No one can say just how long they will last.
Now people can more than just hear how hard it can be.
  Now, so many are starting to feel it themselves unfortunately.
Long lines at the gas stations for gas that's in short supply.
  A long search for formula for the babies, you must try and try.
At the supermarket, some of the shelves are bare.
  Some food that used to be, is no longer there.
A lot of people are feeling the pinch and are finally starting to care.

Hard Times today,
are becoming a big pain I hear people say.
  When hard times get harder,
  it'll be more than the money they'll pay
When some folks start dying from freezing,
the times will be so terribly painful,
while more die from starving.
  The misery experienced so needlessly is so shameful,
  all because of some deranged people with crazy ideas.
Some people in power who will never change,
no matter how many millions give voice to their pleas.
  There's a mission to destroy and totally arrange,
  the once free life we all once knew.
Only if we sit back and allow it, will it come true.

Poem No. 15

Same As It Ever Was

Day to day,
life still starts out the same old way.
　The sun comes up in the East.
It's man against man.
　It's man against beast.
Sometimes it's who has the best plan,
that will in the end eat the feast.

It's a fight for survival they say,
it's the way it's forever been and likely will stay.
　The sun sets in the evening in the West.
Another day is gone.
　The world to comprehend is a monumental test.
When looking back at what we've done,
did we all do what we could to be our best?

People keep making babies among all the fray,
perpetuating the human race while keeping evil at bay.
　The moon has its phases as the earth rotates around the sun.
Our species supposedly changed through evolutions,
at least according to some.
　We still go out and kill each other, sometimes by the millions,
　when back in pre-history, at least it was just one by one.

Technology is evolving at an amazing rate,
and in many ways can make life seem great.
　It makes me think of some of the ways that it's not.
The basic fundamentals I see haven't changed all that much,
I remember some wonderful traditions some have forgot.
　There's always a new crazy idea with too many people out of touch,
　with too many radical activists with a far-out cause.
My long and aged observations conclude this as such,
it's all pretty much the same, same as it ever was.

Poem No. 16
The Crime Rate's Up In River City

That's right folks, right here in River City,
trouble has come to town.
The crime rate's up and it's a real pity.

The conviction rate is way down,
and the streets are getting mean and gritty.
The criminals now, their crimes atrocious and renown.

This isn't some gangster movie, it's for real.
The story's an old one, it's all the same.
The criminals now, know it's one sweet deal.

It's what always happens when you lose control of the game.
It's always been, the good guys against the bad guys, their evil ways to
repeal.
But what we have here in River City is a crime rate that's a real shame.

The policymakers making policy, implementing ideas with the stupidity
they can no longer conceal.
A lame and clueless group with no true emotions or empathy with which
to feel.
At least now we all know the ones that are the ones to blame.

Poem No. 17
It Can Always Get Worse

If you think things are bad right now,
it may be true,
but believe me, there's always somehow,
no matter what you do,
it can always get worse.
   Sometimes it can get so bad, you want to curse.
There may be a heavy rain pouring down,
the streets are flooding, you start wondering if you may drown.
   If it keeps raining you don't know how it could get worse, but it can.
Now you wish you had listened last night to your local weatherman.
   Water's coming in under the door, it's getting to be quite a flow.
If your feet are getting wet, and you don't know whether to stay or go,
you better decide and find somewhere better.
   Or you can stay right there, taking the chance, of only getting wetter.
You might think that this situation is adverse,
 but don't forget, it can always get worse.
   The wind may be howling and sound really fierce,
   but still, be thankful that you don't get hit by a tornado.
That would certainly be worse, anyone would tell you so.
   There are thousands of things that could go wrong, or more,
   just like all those terrible things that have happened before.
If you hang in there when it all hits the fan,
you can be a survivor, tap into your fortitude, you know that you can.
   Don't be a complainer whining about it all day,
   as bad as you may think that it is, and the whole deal perverse,
   better think twice about bailing here, somewhere else can always be
worse.
Sometimes we don't know when we really have it good,
we dream of greener pastures and better days to have if we could.
   All the time, we have what we really need, and should be happy we're
not in the back of a hearse.
Like I've been saying, it can always get worse.

Poem No. 18

Put Them in a Box

There are those who would,
  they've tried heaven knows,
   just as hard as they could.
They want to gather us all into a group,
  divide us up by visual sight.
Assign a designation to divide each troop.
Put them in a box, one that fits just right.
  Put a label on it, make up a dirty name.
Let's pit them against each other, oh what a real fun game.
  Don't dare let them come together,
  no not over anything.
Or we can't be their savior,
  we have to save them from something.
Something, like their differences are bad,
  instead of embracing the differences and being glad.
Individuals trapped in a stereotyping singularity,
  by nature, are destined to go absolutely nowhere,
  as it's meant to be.
As if bound by conscription,
  tied to the most stringent and oppressive rules.
One wonders by any definition,
  who really are the fools?
For all an equal opportunity,
  that's as fair as it can be.
The opportunity for success,
  a means to progress,
  but that doesn't come with any guarantee.
It's up to each person to make it a reality.
Don't be fooled by those that would try to divide,
  their concern is not sincere, they're not on your side.
No one should ever put a label on someone, ...anyone,
  we're all just one species in total, the human race.

(continued on next page)

If only that negative kind of thinking we could erase,
 a "human being", that's the only label, all others should be gone,
  with all attached prejudices, to be gone without a trace.
No one should put anyone in some blatant box,
  put into a category for those who mocks.
Every single person should be regarded with the same respect,
  and have all the rights equal to be whatever they aspire to be.
Not stereotyped by any grouping, labeling, or some throwback
retrospect.
Let all people live their lives as they should, individually and free.
  C'mon, think outside the box, while you introspect.

Don't hang no "jacket" on me.

Poem No. 19
A Horse of a Different Color

It could be an ebony black, or it could be white as snow,
it could be a deep dark brown,
how about a warm tan, something with that soft glow?
  Maybe a bright yellow color that's laying around,
  or some color we don't even yet know.
The color could be like an emerald so shiny green,
maybe a copper with a shiny sheen.
  And it could be a mix of colors, like I have seen.

Sometimes you must stand back,
give it all some slack,
like this easy going, open-minded man.
when it comes to a horse, the color doesn't need to be part of the plan.
  It doesn't really matter to me,
  what color a horse may be,
  because a horse of a different color is still a horse you see.

If I should take a stroll down the street,
and if upon that street I perchance a man to meet,
someone whose skin is much darker than me,
does it matter how much darker it may be?
  It makes no difference that I can see,
  because a man of a different color is still just a man, like me,
  …don't you see?

Poem No. 20
Can Jimmy Come Out to Play?

(doorbell: ring, ring)
"Mrs. Thompson, can Jimmy come out to play?"
"No, I'm sorry Tommy, he has had his shot,
but next week he gets his booster, then he'll be OK."

Next Week: (ring, ring)
"Mrs. Thompson, is it today?
Did Jimmy get his booster, now can he come out to play?"
"Yes, he got his booster, but I'm afraid that inside he must stay.
He has his special N-95 mask, but we're waiting for his face shield,
shipping hit a delay,
but it should be delivered later today."

The Next Day: (ring, ring)
"Mrs. Thompson, is Jimmy going to be able to come out to play?"
"Yes, he can, wait right here,
there's a chill in the air, Jimmy must prepare.
He must put on his sweater and gloves,
oh, and the stocking cap that he loves.
He must of course have his N-95, his cloth mask over that.
Then his face shield, as soon as I remember where it's at.
I'll have him start getting ready now."
"That's OK Mrs. Thompson, I think we'll try and find another 2nd
baseman
somehow."

Poem No. 21
It's Water Under the Bridge

The train has left the station,
that ship has sailed.
 We've been there, done that, we know the situation.
The times we succeeded, the times we failed.
 We've been around the block as they say,
  more than a time or two.
There's a lot to remember from back in the day,
  even though some of it we don't care to.
Recalling all those things that we use to do,
memories, some that are not too great.
 Mistakes made along the way,
  but life's lessons learned before it was too late.
We can be thankful we didn't do any more damage,
  thankful that now, it's water under the bridge.

Young and reckless in our wilder days,
fearless, we were invincible like Superman.
 Ambitious and motivated in so many ways,
  we were working on the great American plan.
Relentless in our pursuit,
we were driven by a burning need.
 We were always looking for the shortest route,
  we were compelled to in any way succeed.
When the bill came due, we paid the price in the end,
for all the shortcuts and rules we bent, and we broke.
 It was deemed justified, or at least that's what we'd pretend.
We knew better, but we cared not, so of it we never spoke.

So, we can dwell on the past and deeds that we've done,
but somehow, we found the right path to happiness in life.
 Now, let bygones be bygones and let them be gone.

(continued on next page)

Memories of bad times can cut you like a knife,
it's best to cut them free and give your mind a message,
  Sweat it not, after all, it shouldn't bother you now,
  after all,... now you can say, it's just water under the bridge.

Poem No. 22

"Push Buttons"

Before that phone call you're about to make,

just a moment would you take?

Reflect if you will about how it is these days,

compared to how it was with the old ways.

Crank, crank!

One ringy dingy, Two ringy dingys,

to whom am I speaking? What number please?

… and then.

It's put a finger in the right numbered hole… give it a spin.

With the next number needed… put a finger in a hole again.

(Click, Click, Click)

As the old rotary dial each time would return,

no longer needing an operator,

unless you were a long distance

caller and you had money to burn.

(Very expensive!)

The only problem was you see, you had all these phone numbers to learn.

Alas, the future finally arrived,

with the glorious new push button phone.

Now barely believing my fingers survived,

from all the dialing, they were sore,

sore to the bone.

After a time, there were cellphones,

and they had push buttons too.

(continued on next page)

Then I could hardly believe it, those phones,
                                    they had memories, it's true!
No more numbers to remember.
What else could a phone possibly do?

Before you knew it,
                        everything had push buttons on it.
Mama's stove, the dishwasher, and her blender,
                                    Papa's radio, and our TV.
Even Grampa's car had a push button transmission,
                                it was plain to see it was a
                                push button revolution.
Now days, the push buttons are gone,   (boy were they hard to push.)
                            the effort it took was almost obscene.
They all in a short time, just seemed to disappear somehow.

All the phones, TV's, PC's, and everything else now,
                                have a touch sensitive screen.
My fingers often hit in the wrong places,
                        I try to text, and I forget to make the spaces.
I give in, it's too tough,
                        and I use to think the old times were so rough.
But that's okay, presently when I make a call,
                            I can talk into my phone,
                            and don't have to use my fingers at all.
The only problem now today,
                            I can never think of what to say.
And now they tell me, I can get the latest thing called 5G,
                            but that doesn't mean a thing to me.

Poem No. 23
When the Dust Settles

When it inevitably hits the fan,
you can try to do all that you can,
but you know nevertheless, it's going to fly.
  When we get speeches that are just a salad of words,
  sounds like somebody must be high.
We have leaders that think they can get by,
with senseless policies, unpopular by more than two-thirds.
  And the crap coming continually down the pike,
  there's not one damn thing I hear that I like.

Talking heads take up your time, they fill up your head,
you don't know if it really happened at all,
or was it somebody's fantasy instead?
  No one knows the number affected, how many took the fall,
  how many were injured, how many were dead.
All a glorious fabrication, a grand pretense,
it's all getting insanely and wildly intense.
what kind of reality is this here? Nothing makes sense.

Before all the missiles and bombs have gone off,
will someone stand up, and finally say enough is enough?
  Until that day,
  when perhaps I pray, we can find some way.
Maybe when the dust settles, so many more will see,
war is senseless, relentless, and a crime against humanity.
  I wonder how many more must die so needlessly,
  just collateral damage in this desperate travesty.
The causes of which, and the motivation,
 greed, a lust for power, and deep corruption,
  … wrapped up with a whole lot of stupidity!

(continued on next page)

It would be so great,
if someday before it was too late,
maybe by some great magical force yet unknown to me.
  For that's what it would take,
  to correct humankind's big mistake,
  and war would become obsolete,
  and just become part of history.
On that day,
all our hate would fade away.
  Some say though, that I live constantly,
  in a fantasy.

Poem No. 24
Any Day Now

Any day now,
… it could be real soon.
  Any day now,
… we could be mining green cheese on the moon.
On that day, everyone will be singing the same tune.
  Any day now,
  …we could be freezing in the middle of June.

Any day,… it could go either way,
up or down, left, or right,
but I'm pretty sure I'll never see the day,
when there's anything anywhere in between.
  There will be nowhere within that plight,
  no true compromise will ever be seen.

Any day,... pick any one you would like.
  What would you like to do?
  Maybe you could cruise out of town on your silly motor bike.
You know you have to do what you have to,
for, … any day now,
everyone could tell you, they're done with you, so take a hike.

Any day now,
…anything at all can go down,
  At any time, it could always come back up, anyhow.
It could come up so high and get so deep, we could drown.
  Where can one stand, and not be in the way,
  and when was just standing around okay?

Any day,… It could all go away.
  It could be today,

(continued on next page)

in an instant, instantly gone.
It could be you that goes, so live life well,
before it's all over, and your time is done.
   I know you don't want to reside in Hell.
So, be loving and kind, do good and you'll be okay.
   Think about what your life's actions have to say,
Maybe you shouldn't wait,
… you never know, it could be any day.

Poem No. 25
"Watchers" from Afar

This is a world with so many countries,
a world with so many kinds of people.
> So many people living their good lives,
> as time relentlessly passes by.

All these good people are what they are,
while they watch from afar,
the world of others crumbling,
somehow they forget how to cry.

In a faraway land, an evil madman has gone wild,
so many are ruthlessly and needlessly dying.
The murderers are seen on TV everywhere, every day,
in the tanks they're driving.
> Searching for any man, woman, or child,
> that may still be somehow surviving.

Every day and night they can sit and watch fiery missiles fall like rain,
indiscriminately upon the poor people of Ukraine.
> While "Watchers" from lands far away watch,
> and stand back, watching, standing idly by.

After all, I guess it's not so hard,
when it's not their loved ones they're watching die!

So many cry out for the sake of humanity,
Still, no one will do what it will demand,
to put a stop to this madness and insanity.
> Just who in the Hell is in command?
> The world's watching a horrible catastrophe,
> everyone needs to take up the cause and take a stand.

I wonder how much longer the leaders of the civilized world will linger,
how much longer would they just sit and watch, what would it take, what
would be enough?

(continued on next page)

Would they finally be moved to action, and choose not to just watch any longer,
if it was their women and children getting raped, and their legs blown off,
would that be enough?
How many more, how high the death toll?
            What must the numbers be before,
            the world will stop only watching, this horror show?

Who'll be the needed leader that will step up and step in?
Be a hero, do the world a favor,
bring this evil war to an end!
            You can say it doesn't matter or bother you,
            or you can just watch, … and pretend.
The world should not allow such atrocities to go on and on.
The world is united in its shared revulsion,
but still the carnage continues, and the evil mad man is still not done.
Some wonder why the wait, we need some united offensive action,
…let's put the enemy on the run.

Poem No. 26
Crawling Back in My Hole

It's dark, but not too dark,
and it's warm.
  Insulated very well, a cozy place to park.
It's built strongly to weather a storm.
  It's a place in my mind to protect my sanity and soul,
  somewhere to get away from all the hate and division.
My sanctuary to where I can be in control.
  With all this confusion and dissention,
  I need a safe place to go,
  I give up, … I'm crawling back in my hole.

Out there in the wide open, there's no protection,
it's tough being a human being.
  Just prey, subject to the laws of natural selection.
With problems and pressures growing,
there seems no end in sight.
  No matter how hard we try, and we do try,
  it looks like we just can't get it right.
We need to get it together as a community,
we that want to call ourselves civilized humanity.
  No one cares any longer if you live or die,
  the lack of compassion and empathy makes me want to cry.
So many it seems, lack integrity and any class.
  Our values long ago, someone came along and stole.
The world can kiss my ass,
and you can tell them I said so.
  I've had it, … I'm crawling back in my hole.

Always be careful what you wish for; some wished for a lot.
The world is such a mess, a real bonified catastrophe,
due to some solid principles and common sense somebody forgot.

(continued on next page)

Some people got lazy,
   thinking life for them should be easy.
Where is that Utopia that's supposed to be?
   That's what I heard, that's what was promised to me,
   but every day it gets harder and harder to maintain.
I'm fed up with this whole damn scene,
it's just too much, an overload for my frazzled brain.
   I no longer want to choose, left, right, or in between.
Everyone can just leave me alone, I'm tired of playing the role.
   I really don't need this crap; so, … I'm crawling back in my hole.

Poem No. 27
With Pen in Hand

With pen in hand, the old masters wrote the classics for prosperity.
They often wrote with great precision and uncomplicated clarity.
With pen in hand, they crafted words to tell,
a story, an emotion, a vision, which could put you under a spell.
Words captured on paper to express wisdom of the ages,
the recognition of which, did slowly come in stages.
Their poems, their plays, and all their stories,
across the land they did widely cast,
these poets, these authors of the past.

With laptop and keyboard close at hand,
these days I sit, and I ponder.
Mysteries abound to explore, and I try to understand,
all of life, and this wide world of wonder.
With laptop and a mouse that I can click to enter,
the words that today I contemplate,
in seconds can be printed out automatically on center.
Now my words I can widely disseminate,
… electronically,
there on a "cloud" for all the world to see,
… and it's all done …quite instantly!

Poem No. 28

Belle's Saloon

The trail was dusty, me with my bandana pulled up tight,
I'm riding my trusty horse and I see a familiar cactus off to the right.
  Knowing then I only had a few more miles to go,
  I could feel my horse's anticipation begin to grow,
  he knew what waited there as well as I did.
So, the pace was picked up and we went galloping ahead.
  Just beyond that near-by ridge I'll be able to see,
  the sight of the town of Tombstone where soon we will be.
It's going to be another hot Arizona afternoon,
and as soon as I can I'll be standing at the bar in Belle's Saloon.

Belle's a very classy lady with some good business sense.
  She came out west 10 years ago, a woman of no pretense.
All the way from Boston town where once she had a hattery.
  The finest hats for the ladies until she was arrested for assault and
battery.
There was a gentleman caller who wasn't like a gentleman at all.
  Belle quickly with her knee put him in his place,
  but the gentleman was a lawyer and Belle had to take a fall.
1 year later she was free to go but with her disgrace,
no shop or inventory did she retain.
  With a little money stashed away, she started thinking of where
  should she try starting over again.
Out west, people talk of all the fantastic opportunities out there.

When Belle hit town and she looked around,
her face developed a scowl and a frown.
  She stood there now in front of the town's town hall,
  she didn't see much of a market for fine ladies' hats at all.
Upon a tour of the town there was a sign she found,
outside of an old dry goods store, said it was for sale.

(continued on next page)

A visit to the bank where the title was held,
   yielded Belle the place paid in full, she could only pray she wouldn't fail.
She knew the town was full of mining men and cattlemen and money to be made,
figuring her chances would be very good if here she stayed.
   Her place was on the main drag, right on Allen Street,
   seemed like it was somewhere everyone liked to congregate and meet.
With some long days of cleaning and painting,
decorating and some major renovating.
   Belle finally hung up her sign for her new business.
It didn't take long and it became a big success.
   When it came to the name of the place, she kept it simple and short,
   "Belle's Saloon" that's good enough, that'll do I heard her report.
Now a half past noon,
finally arriving here after riding all the way from Dragoon.
   After eating all that dust along the way,
   I'm standing at the bar and here I'll stay.
Waiting for a cold one, hoping it gets here soon,
then I'll be just another happy cowboy hanging out in Belle's Saloon.

Photo by author

Poem No. 29
Early Morning Sunlight

Soon after sunrise,
 After some coffee, and I've opened up my eyes.
I stroll out to the patio,
 I'm looking for that spot,
The one that's warm with a golden glow.
 Soothing and pleasant, and not too hot.
While a gentle morning breeze begins to blow,
 I know I've found the spot that's just right,
Where I will contemplate what I shall do today.
 Here in my sunny spot in this early morning sunlight,
Sometimes I think it's the best part of my day.

Photo by author

Poem No. 30
Heavy Rain

Hanging across the western sky ahead,
it seems like molten lead.
A gray so dark, before it turns to black.
The sun's been gone so long …is it dead?
Will it ever come back?
The thoughts weigh heavy with each rain drop that falls.
Sheets of rain now look like gray steel walls.
Across the vast valley landscape laid out before me,
in the sky great lightning streaks flash chaotically.
Temporary illumination, then the darkness wins back the night,
as the thunder rolls across the land sporadically,
the vibrations fill the air, and I feel the storms mighty might.

It's a heavy rain we have here tonight.
It's blocking out the stars and moonlight.
The rain is falling in volumes that is hard to believe.
It leaves one wandering, will it ever leave?
With the rain so heavy as the wind howls on,
the mood is heavy too, while we wait for the storm to be gone.
But in the shelter of our little prairie home,
we are thankful that we are not alone.
We have one another to keep us safe and warm.
Our love and devotion to protect each other from harm.
So, let the rain be heavy as it wants to be,
with my love for you and yours for me,
we'll stick together and we'll stay afloat.
If that doesn't work, we'll build a boat!

Poem No. 31
All Alone… Waiting for a Train

(I believe it was late October, the winter rains had begun… and I was knowing another unhappy "ending", I had lost the sun.)

Waiting for a train,
   waiting in the rain.
Under clouds so dark and gray,
  on a chilly Autumn day.
It fits the mood,
  as I wait to leave here for good.
I stayed too long,
  looks like I got it all wrong,
   her love for me was not that strong.
So, I'm waiting for a train,
  as I watch the water run down the drain.
I'm running it all through my brain,
 but when it's no good anymore,
  and you find it's not what you had before.
When you get home, there's no longer any love in store,
  it's time to move on,
   to be "colored gone".
Sometimes you just have to call it done,
 this run is now complete,
  another love relationship now obsolete.
Take a bus, a plane,
  or like me, you can be,
   on your way, somewhere away,
   and be waiting on a train.
I'm leaving like the leaves leaving the trees,
 losing all my stress and my anxieties.
I'm waiting in the rain,
  thinking about what could have been,
   then thinking about being all alone again,

(continued on next page)

as I feel the pain of the heartbreak really kick in.
Now I'm looking for a warmer clime,
  and a better, gentler, happier time.
Wondering about if I'll ever find someone,
  and find true love and happiness in the end.
Loneliness is a bitch, so painful when you have no one,
  as I feel the cold emptiness start to descend.

Poem No. 32
When Our Ship Comes In

We're just waiting on the day,
while we're busy looking for that better way.
  We're working hard for those American dreams,
   it just keeps getting harder every day it seems.
Every year that comes gets tougher,
life's long road gets a little rougher.
  But we'll keep knocking it out,
   keeping the faith, we'll have no doubt.
Any day now the good life could begin,
at last, when our ship comes in.

We may be called dreamers, that's okay.
  We have something to look forward to everyday.
It's something to keep us going,
something to keep the juices flowing,
it's far better than being without hope,
far better if you have something to help you cope.
  You shouldn't have a negative view,
   maybe you don't know it, that can be bad for you.
You'll always be a loser if you don't think you'll ever win,
you'll see we can be winners, when our ship comes in.

While some may keep whining about how it's not fair,
we'll keep thinking of how we can get somewhere.
  Although we keep talking of all the things we'll do,
   we're not just sitting around waiting for our dreams to come true.
Sometimes it requires some effort, sometimes some sacrifice.
  One needs to put in the work, and you shouldn't think twice.
You need to make it happen if you want to win that big prize.
  It's time to wake up and realize,

(continued on next page)

  you've got to be the captain of that ship, now's a good time to begin.
We're sure it's going to be smooth sailing to the end,
until then,
we'll just keep treading water,
waiting for when our ship comes in.

Poem No. 33
We're Holding On

There's a knock in the engine of our old car.
If we need to get somewhere,
we don't know if we'll get very far.
  Maybe we'll make it on prayer,
  or a wish on a falling star.
The baby has the colic, the older boy has the flu.
  Meanwhile, the wife got laid off and she doesn't know what she'll do.
Our refrigerator has a rattle when it's running,
the A/C keeps running but with a real loud humming,
and it's not keeping the house very cool.
  I'm in the backyard spraying down with a garden hose,
  I'm not quite naked, but I'm pretty damn close.
My next-door neighbor is looking at me like I'm a fool,
standing there in my underwear.
  We can hope that our troubles will soon disappear,
  the hard times will finally be gone.
Until then though… we're holding on.

There may be plenty that we haven't got,
but when it comes to love and devotion, we have a lot.
  Together with each other, we find the strength to endure,
  for we have that bond of family that's pure.
We take on the challenges of life together,
united unbroken forever.
  No matter what, we'll find a way,
  one day at a time somehow we'll get through the day.
I was never told that it was going to be easy,
so I never expected too much to be free.
  Sometimes it takes some hard work admittedly.
Sometimes, you just need to be able to face reality,
as hard as it may be.

(continued on next page)

Tomorrow today's trouble may be just a bygone memory,
we could win the lottery.
Until then we're happy to be doing okay…
"We're holding on"… at least we are today.
Unfortunately, that's more than some folks can say.

51

Poem No. 34
Watching the Waves Wash in

One after one,
I'm watching everyone.
  Laying here on the beach in the sand,
  drinking a Margarita until it's gone.
Mixing up another one to put in my hand.
  I'm watching the waves wash in,
  letting the sun bake my skin.

One and then another,
they keep coming one after the other.
  My mind's at ease,
  let this calm last a lot longer please.
It's so funny how my troubles seem to cease,
they seem to fade away again and again,
with each wave I watch wash in.

One after one,
I hear the rhythm as they rush on.
  Bashing against the rocky shore,
  one wave rushes in then it's gone.
A wave colliding, then one more, then one more,
spraying the air with that salty sea.
  I could stay for hours and when they asked where I'd been,
  I wouldn't stutter I'd say, I've been taking it easy,
  just watching the waves wash in.

Poem No. 35
Beach Shack

There on a white sandy shore,
 a shack, a little hut, nothing more, but so much more.
  The bluest ocean, its waves crashing in upon the beach.
There're so many wonderful things within my reach.
  The clean ocean breeze, the nice warm sun, peace, and solitude.
 It's always the best medicine to adjust my attitude.
  The beach shack,
  every time I leave, I can't wait to get back.
It's my one place that I can get back on track.

There's just one room with a loft,
  I sleep there on a cozy bed so soft.
There's a great big window that looks out at the water,
 it takes up most of the wall, but I wish it were bigger.
  At night, the waves reflect the moonlight,
  as I sit around the firelight.
I gaze up at a gazillion stars in the clear night sky.
  I sit there in my serenity, and I have to wonder why,
  what could be better than laying here feeling a natural high.

There's multi-million-dollar mansions sitting high on a cliff,
  I don't care about that at all because there's one great big diff,
  they are down the beach about a mile or two,
  with all their HOA rules and every month, a costly fee is due.
Sitting on little plots of land about the size of a postage stamp.
  It wouldn't be enough room for me, I think my legs would start to
cramp.
So, here's the thing, it's obviously true,
here I have plenty of space and privacy, and I can do what I want to do.
  Besides all this and more, I have a much better view.

Poem No. 36
Push and Pull

Push and pull, what a tug of war.
  What we aren't and what we are.
Back and forth, around, and around it goes.
  Where it all will end up, nobody knows.

Billy wants a dog and Sally wants a cat.
  Everybody wants an answer, and no one knows where it's at.
There's plenty that they do know, unfortunately none of it's true.
  Someone's always wanting to lay a trip on you.

Martin wants a Mercedes, but Eleanor wants a Lexus.
  Going back and forth over dinner, and money was one of the causes.
They could afford only one car payment; they couldn't handle two.
  Not wanting to compromise, they got divorced, for them there was
nothing left to do.

Some people want to push you to the left.
  Some people want to pull you to the right.
After all the pushing and pulling the truth may be seen.
  It won't be at either end, but somewhere in between.

Poem No. 37
Down in the Valley Below

There is a valley that lies between mountains so high.
  I can't paint you a picture, but with my words I will try.
Below a brilliant topaz and partly cloudy sky,
I hear a rushing mountain stream with its waters roaring by.
  Down the trail a ways, I listen to the quiet and hear myself sigh.
A sigh of relief, now to my stress and tensions I can say good-bye.
  Down in the valley below,
  where often I like to go.
There with its crisp clean air,
and all the tall evergreen trees everywhere.
  Wild-flowers bloom in the spring, summer and into the fall,
  while I'm always amazed at the sheer beauty of it all.
There's wildlife plenty in this valley within its woods that roam,
deer, elk, and antelope along with bears and others call this valley home.
  Down in this valley where I watch the squirrels and rabbits play,
  a stroll amongst nature, I can't think of a better way to start my day.

(continued on next page)

Here, down in the valley, it's a place of serenity I find,
here, it's so easy to achieve a greater peace of mind.
  Sometimes one should take the time for a time-out,
  maybe a time and place to re-assess and figure it out.
While there's this place of mine that I know,
you should look and find, your own valley below,
and for your own sanity,
there you should now and then go.

Poem No. 38

Snow on the Catalina Mountains

Walking out my back door this morning,
I looked up at the mountains, the Catalina mountains,
from my backyard point of view.
　Up there I could see the snow was still falling,
　with the mountain peaks covered by clouds, the darkest gray blue.
The mountain sides, the valleys, and the ravines,
they were all covered in a thick blanket of white.
　Nature was displaying such a panorama of picturesque scenes,
　the sun shining on patches of snow with reflections so bright.
But beyond the beauty I see up there,
it leaves me with a great chill down my spine,
I can almost feel the coldness in the air.
　But I console myself by knowing I'll be just fine,
　I'll be staying nice and warm, and staying down here.
So, let the snow keep falling, as long as it stays up there.

With the old North wind howling down into the valley,
bringing with it its frigid winter air,
as the coldness is penetrating and beginning to get to me.
　I start to wonder, how much longer until the snow finally gets to
　here,
　as I look at my shovel and how much sidewalk I have to clear.
But then I remember, winters and living in Tucson, Arizona,
it won't be too hard to bear,
　Not like it was in the small farmer's town of Monona,
　when I was a kid living back there in good old Iowa.
We used to get blizzards and temps that dipped way below zero,
to wake up in the morning, looking out the frosted window,
at over four feet of white powdery snow.
　Once the snow starts to snow here,
　two hours later, after the sun comes up,
　it will melt, and no longer be there.

Poem No. 39

Monsoons over Arizona

I'm living here in Tucson, Arizona, it's the first week of July.
  What Spring we had, really did fly,
  and it left us pretty high and dry.
The month of May was just here, and too soon,
just like my birthday month of June,
… it was gone.
  Here comes the Sun, and the real heat is coming on,
  those nice warm days and cool nights are over and done.
First 105 degrees or more, that's getting pretty hot.
  Next comes sweltering humidity we almost forgot,
  there're a few clouds over the mountains, but not a lot.
There're monsoon storms are building down south in Mexico.
  It won't be long until they're here over Tucson though,
  the clouds will be building over the Catalina's, the Santa Rita's,
  and the Rincon's, we'll watch them lift high and grow.
With the arrival of the rain the washes will flow,
at times almost daily, well into September,
and maybe even into October,
you just never know!

Sometimes the storms form up north on the Mogollon Rim.
  Sometimes they move this far south, sometimes the chances are great,
  at times they're slim.
When chances are great, the storms will fill the rivers and washes,
sometimes beyond the brim.
  Upon occasion, the storms from the north,
  meet with those from the south,
  right above the city, a supercharged spectacle is brought forth.
The rain shall soon in heavy sheets begin to fall.
  Down into the valley the storms will come with thunder,
  lightning, hail, the wind, and it all.

(continued on next page)

Great bolts of electrical might, across the sky will crack.
  Roaring waves of thunder providing a glorious soundtrack,
  somewhat fading, then hearing the echo come rumbling back.

The washes will be running full or maybe more.
  People will be in the streets dancing and rejoicing by the score,
  like they never saw it rain in their life before.
In the desert, rain is always something needed and good.
  Often times we get too much, too fast, and we have a flood,
  we'd sure like to store it up for dry times though if we could.
After the rain, everywhere one looks, instead of brown, we see all green.
  The wildflowers and the cacti are in full bloom, the colors are keen,
  they're painting such a bright and cheerful, joyful scene.
But the dry earth is thirsty and will soak it all up real soon.
  We here in Arizona like our days sunny, but will change our tune,
  when the dirt gets dry and dusty, we'll be hoping for the return,
  of our blessed life giving, our amazing seasonal Arizona monsoon.

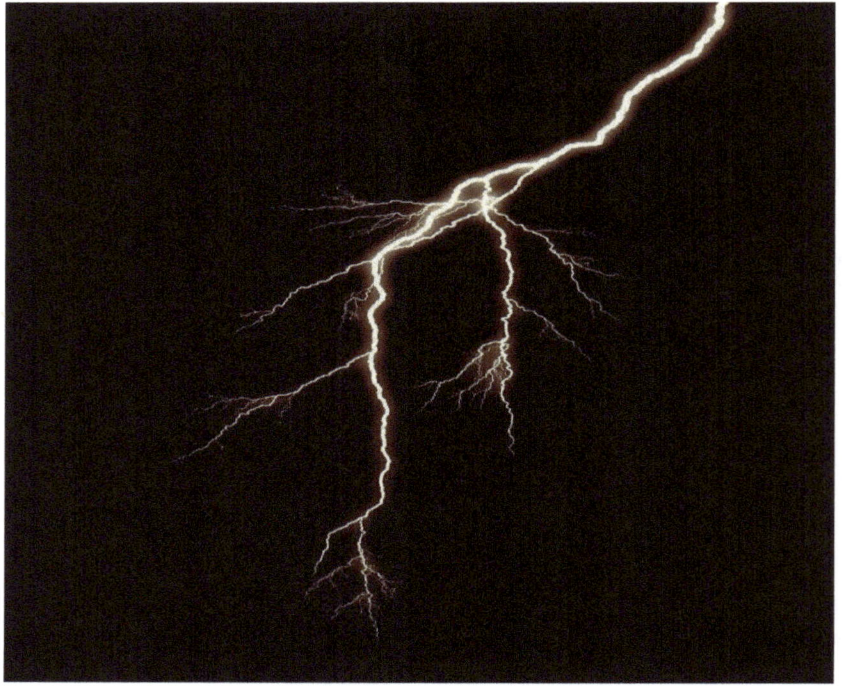

Poem No. 40

Desert Wildflowers

I walked outside in my yard this morning.
A cool morning breeze was gently blowing,
making my good feeling now almost complete.
Looking down, there at my feet,
I saw a small burst of bright orange flowers growing.
Looking around, I could stay here and look for hours.
My eyes took in the different colors of all the wildflowers,
the desert was displaying,
with all its glory showing.
My feelings, I felt so full, there was no denying.
Their bright beauty set my spirit glowing,
my inspirations went flying.

I leaned over and picked a few flowers.
A careful collection of all the colors,
the orangest oranges, the brightest yellows,
a few flowers of blue,
a dark brilliant hue.
Some pretty deep purples and little white wild daisies.
I made a multi-colored bouquet,
to my eyes a sight that so pleases,
a gift from nature that really made my day.
I know they all have a specific scientific name,
the likes of which I cannot say,
but I love my lovely desert wildflowers just the same

Poem No. 41
I Wonder Why

I wonder about a lot.
I wonder about many things,
many people seem to have forgot.
I don't know where some things went wrong,
but hate shouldn't be this strong.
We're supposed to be civilized and able to get along.
When I see millions of people die that don't really need to die,
I wonder why.

I see the conflicts and their reasons,
around the world and throughout the seasons.
I hear all kinds of excuses and explanations,
they all fall short in my mind of any real justifications.
When one believes one way, another believes another.
It doesn't matter if it's a stranger or a brother,
seems as if one just cannot respect the other.
Thoughts and beliefs are supposed to be free,
so why can't some just let everyone be?
I say believe what you want to,
as long as you don't bother me.
But there are those who will always try,
they can't keep it to themselves, and constantly,
I wonder why.

Political positions,
within and between the nations.
Too many countries with plans of territorial aggression.
Plans for ultimately world control and domination.
Not satisfied with what they have, they crave more.
Some want to take it all from you,
they're good at it, they've done it many times before.

(continued on next page)

Political and religious types want you to think what they want you to.
Power and control come with numbers; they want to recruit you.
Being obedient followers and some people do.
Perhaps possessing a deaf ear and a blind eye...
and I wonder why.

Maybe we think we're civilized, but we're not ... in my mind, not by a long shot.
Where can our redemption and forgiveness be sought?
Sorry patrons, looks like so many are lost and have forgot.
To so many God is dead,
an inconvenient obligation they had grown to dread.
I wonder why...
Why so much division,
It seems no one can see eye to eye.
So many seek revision,
no matter how hard they try,
the good changes never seem to fly.
Some of it just makes me want to cry.
While some people wonder why I wonder,
sometimes ...I too, wonder why.

Poem No. 42
A Wingless Dreamer

(Stepfather) "Get your head out of the clouds boy!"
(Mother) "You're just a daydreamer, you'll never amount to anything, boy"

I was that boy.
Being a farmer's stepson was a hard life, not a lot of fun.
Hard work, long hours, it was hard to find much joy,
doing chores all day long, 8 years of school was over and done.
Now, I was bucking bales of hay in the hot summer sun.

Imagination was my only escape that I could find.
It served me well whenever I could find the time.
I'd get away from it all completely, by just using my mind.
But should I be caught daydreaming; it was treated like a crime.

With my flights of fancy, I could let my mind soar to lofty heights.
I could fly among the clouds without the aid of any wings.
I was like a wingless dreamer with visions of beauty within my sights,
My soul would take it all in, and all the wonder such a feeling brings.

My dreaming could take me anywhere I wanted to go,
anywhere in this world, with no limits in time or place.
I could be anyone I wanted to be, no one could tell me no.
Free in my dreams, my grandest ambitions I could embrace.

Even though admonished by my parents for doing so,
it was compulsive, and I would not, could not stop.
Trapped in a rural kind of servitude scenario,
my dreams could take me from my dreary bottom,
to some fantastic mountain top.

(continued on next page)

My dreams as I became older became goals for me to strive for.
Settling for next to nothing on the farm, was never an option for me,
so, I worked hard because I kept dreaming you see,
of being something more.
I'm so glad I had my dreams to explore,
… that I had dreams to make a reality.

Throughout this life, many of those daydreams once had when I was younger,
with determination and commitment, I have seen those dreams come true for me.
The desire to see my dreams come true was the motivation that made me stronger.
That's who I am, without any wings, but still soaring high, and I will always be,
what I've always been, forevermore, a very blessed and thankful "Wingless Dreamer".

Poem No. 43
Things I Don't Do Anymore

I don't drink Jack Daniels by the bottle anymore.
My 2nd home isn't the neighborhood bar like before.
I don't get into bar room fights, the bruises hurt so much more.
Now days, I don't need to get beat up to feel sore.

I don't drive the Mustang any longer at 125,
I love my car and myself, and I'm now concerned we both survive.
When headed for a destination I want to be certain that I arrive,
at this older age, suddenly it's become more important to stay alive.

I don't go out chasing women anymore,
and they've stopped chasing me like they used to before.
I'm long time happily married, coming up, anniversary No. 34,
Thankful, no longer having to look for some way to score.

I no longer stay out until the crack of dawn,
these days I'm in bed with the curtains drawn,
I'm fast asleep before the 10:00 o'clock news comes on.
I need 8 hours of solid rest before next I see the sun.

I don't go out and play baseball with the boys,
the back just can't take the strain these days.
A lot of things I don't do now are just faded joys,
to do them now would hurt me in so many ways.

I don't do too much that's of the physical kind,
In most cases it's too damn dangerous to this old body of mine I find.
These days I live more cautiously and try to be more relaxed and refined.
And now days, not so many people think I'm totally out of my mind.

Poem No. 44

Work

Some call it work and say it like a dirty word.
  Some don't like it much, some do I've heard.
Work if you like yours, ain't really work I guess,
  But it's work if you hate yours, you may as well confess.

If you work for a living,
  Then your work is your life it's giving.
Would you rather not work at all, wouldn't that be nice?
  Let someone else do the work and pay the price.

Let someone else take the fall,
  If it doesn't work out well at all.
It must be they didn't work hard enough to take care of you.
  It couldn't be your fault, there was nothing you thought you could do.

So, watch the work get done by those who know,
  Work is a wonderful thing that makes everything flow.
It's something to take pride in when done well.
  Work, if you can dig it, isn't it swell?

Poem No. 45
Autumn Leaves

Glorious gold, bright yellow & red,
　So gently gliding as they fall.
The Aspen & Maple it is said,
　Is the brightest of them all.
Silent messengers of what's coming.
　Winter is coming and it's near.
Soon the old North Wind will be howling,
　Then the autumn leaves will soon be gone.
Winter w/ its snow to cover them will be here.
　Mother Nature's will, will be done.
But on a nice warm fall day,
　It's so wonderful to just enjoy this colorful array,
Oh, how I wish these beautiful autumn leaves could stay.

Poem No. 46

Go Fly A Kite

If you're not feeling quite right, maybe you're a bit uptight.
Here's one thing you might do, go outside beneath the sky so blue,
… and go fly a kite!
Watch it as it takes flight, as it rides the waves of air.
While you watch it darting chaotically here and there.
Let your mind wander too, think thoughts of better days gone by.
And think of better days coming to you, as you watch your kite fly
… and in an azure blue sky, soaring so high.
Let the wind lift your kite, and your spirits as well,
Remember, the rest of your story is yet to tell.
So, try to keep your goals in sight, but remember to keep your stress level light.
And, every now and then, you should just give in,
… and go fly a kite.

Poem No. 47
To Ease the Pain

Upon my good name,
  it became a stain.
The total misuse of my brain,
  doing stupid stuff over and over again and again.
Everything that I did, seemed to go against the grain.
  Wanting some relief from the emotional drain.
But all I ever did; I did to ease the pain.

I had my chances I cannot lie,
  every time I let them pass me by.
Looking in the wrong places,
  for answers to questions, I didn't even know.
Waking up to stranger's faces,
  just so the pain of loneliness would go.
When they're gone, there's nothing left again,
  and I still want something to ease the pain.

Many days and nights spent searching.
  Sometimes to the bottle I'd be reaching,
    sometimes something to stick in my arm somewhere.
A magic pill in my mouth makes me think I'm not even here.
  If I don't exist,
    the pain can no longer persist.
Then maybe I could finally refrain,
  and no longer would have to have anything to ease the pain.

Though in the here and now,
 presently I must find somehow,
  to break free.
To be independent you see.

(continued on next page)

Whatever is causing this hurting constantly,
  I must fight and win my own personal victory.
A person can't keep feeling hurt again and again.
  I had to find a way my pain to appease,
   not from the outside but from within.
To no longer have any pain that I had to ease,
  I could be happy with the life I'm in,
  no longer needing or wanting anything!... to ease the pain.

The answer I needed to find,
  I found buried deep within my mind.
  Self-examination led me to see,
   realistic expectations and realizing that life has no guarantee.
Within me I found the strength to maintain my sanity,
  finding the true nature of me, and how to be happy,
  with just being me.

Poem No. 48
Step Up

When it falls on you, what will you do?
  Can you handle the pressure, can you remain true,
  or like a piece of paper fold?
Like with no spine your shoulders to hold.
  Don't go down so easily, sometimes you must stand up.
If there's a job to do, you have to step up.
  Get in there, you can get it done,
  clear your mind of doubt.
Let all that be gone,
keep trying until you work it out.

When we put forth an effort that is sincere,
with some talent and perseverance, we can get there.
  To some place in life where we can proudly say,
  "Here is what I've accomplished" and I did it my way.
Never sell yourself short or your potential,
a little faith in you is kind of essential.
  When next you are handed a challenge to meet,
  don't automatically give up and admit defeat.
Be forever steadfast and never give up,
at least you will know you tried your best,
and when the time came you were willing to step up.
  Then you'll pass one of life's most important tests.

Poem No. 49
Roll On

When life smacks you right in the face,
you have to roll with the punch.
   Get right back up and in your place,
   don't let the bullies take your lunch.
You don't have to take it anymore,
it's no longer the way it was before.
   Just because the opposition's voices may be loud,
   stand up, be counted, and be proud.
Hold fast to the spirit that's in you my friend,
today is only the beginning, not the end.
   I know it's far from dead and gone,
   so, my friend… let's roll on.

Let us greet each new day,
in a positive optimistic sort of way.
   Let troubles of yesterday become a distant past,
   don't let them drag you down letting the misery last.
Each day is a new opportunity,
we can make it whatever we want it to be.
   Have faith and be confident in yourself,
   don't ever be satisfied with just sitting on the shelf.
Nothing tried leaves something unsatisfied,
if they say it'll get you somewhere, they lied.
   Maybe you should get off your can before the day is gone,
   let's get fired up man… and let's roll, roll on and on.

Poem No. 50
Cabin Fever

I have a house with 3 rooms, each with 4 walls,
With 1 bathroom and 2 halls.
  Everywhere I look it's 4 walls I see.
I look out the windows and see the same scenery.
  I can't go out-
  there's a nasty flu bug about.
The flu can give you a fever-
but staying in so you don't get it ever,
this can give you a fever of a different kind.
  A fever that permeates the mind.
People call it "Cabin Fever" and I've got it bad.
  I can't get a signal for my cellphone, and I think I'm going mad,
  the satellite TV is down, but with all the bad news on, I'm almost glad.
In a day or 2 they're forecasting 3 feet of snow,
if I don't jump in the truck soon, I won't be able to go.
  I'd have to figure a way around the wildfires though.

(continued on next page)

I listened intently to the evening news on my radio,
to see if they'd know,
is this ugly "bug" an epidemic,
or will it soon be a pandemic?
  All they said was we'll have to wait and see.
Meanwhile that's no comfort and no help to me.
  I don't mean to be all whiny and bitchy,
  it' just that my feet are growing itchy.
If I don't get out of here soon,
I may turn into a complete loony toon.
  So, here I sit with no escape plan clear,
  wishing that they had the 5G network here.
In a few days when I get snowed in,
I could use my phone to get air-lifted somewhere.
  And never come back here again.

Poem No. 51
We Played Monopoly

Back where I was born, back in the hills,
there weren't many thrills,
… but there were some.
  My family didn't own a T.V. until I was 9.
A neighbor traded Daddy for 2 head of swine.
  Back in those days, trading was better than paying with money.
  my old man always thought not paying any taxes was funny.
The television became a conversation piece,
 with no power for the T.V. it wasn't much good back then.
We didn't get electricity to the house until I turned ten.
  But there were always all kinds of things to do,
  we never had time to get bored or blue.
There were chores in the morning and chores at night.
  There was school in between, we had to learn to read and write.
We had running water, but here's what that meant,
running outside to the pumphouse is where you went.
  And when you had to go
  …you know,
  it's outside to the outhouse, for your session to be spent.

Knowing nothing of video games,
no one had had that dream so far.
 We only knew a few famous names,
 and everyone was a movie or country western star.
Excitement mostly came on the weekends,
the family would go fishing or on a picnic in the early springtime sun.
  Playing hide and seek in the dark with my friends,
  climbing trees, building forts, running free, and having fun.
We were kids back then my brothers and I,
kids were meant not to be heard and seldom seen.

(continued on next page)

  We had to entertain ourselves with our imagination, we had to use our
brain.
In those times it's true we didn't have much but that was okay.
  For all we didn't have back in the day, with all that we have today,
  we were just as happy,
  happier maybe some might say.
We were just getting by as one big happy family,
and every Saturday we'd all get together and play Monopoly.

Poem No. 52
Misty Mountain Morning

Like a fine vapor the mist of the morning rises,
softly, so softly shifting, floating in the air,
a light moist envelope that softly encompasses,
like a thin gossamer that's barely there.
  Here in this green covered valley between tall mountain peaks,
  I walk among the towering trees of Pine and Spruce.
Here on this early misty mountain morning, I can find the peace one seeks.
My mind becomes at ease, and I keep my thoughts light and loose,
enjoying nature and Her wonders, such a delight, this sweet, welcomed solitude.
…For I like to adjust my attitude,
  a shift in my mood, at a higher altitude.

I rest my body upon an ancient fallen tree.
  I sit and I ponder and reflect on how I wish things could be.
Alone with my thoughts and feelings of peaceful tranquility,
wishing I could scoop up some of it and take it back home with me.
(continued on next page)

Here there's no stress to be known.
Among the wildflowers in bloom with bright cheerful colors grown,
I can feel all my stress just melt away,
as I watch down by a rushing stream, two young antelope at play.
   I feel so alive and free, it's a shame I can't build me a shack here and
stay.

As the sun continues to rise higher in the clear cerulean sky,
so does the mist begins to lift and disappear when it gets too high.
   A little sad to see it go,
   for unfortunately this is my signal and I know,
   the morning will soon like the mist be gone.
I'll need to be on my way, there's work to get done.
   One more last look before like the mist, I too must be going,
   I'll take the images with me of all this misty mountain beauty,
Although it's at last time to go, I'll take it in, all that nature is showing,
and thank Mother Nature you see,
for all this blessed peace and serenity.

Poem No. 53

Among the Trees

I sat upon a dark green carpet of grass with pen and pad in hand.
It was there among the trees at the edge of the tree line,
I was surveying the valley, such a serene and peaceful stretch of land.
I was there alone and the only thoughts there were mine.
As I sat among the trees,
I began to reflect on these.
I could look left and right, there were plenty trees to see.
As I looked at them individually, I saw quite a variety.
I saw the Maples, Elms, Oaks and a Cottonwood grove very near.
I counted a few Cedar trees that in the winter have branches that are never bare.
Trees I can regard like good silent friends that don't mind listening to me.
I can say what I want, as loud as I can, and none of the trees there will care.
As I sit among the trees as I often do, I can talk of how I would like things to be.
I can dream my wildest dreams; the trees don't mind.
I can rant and rave sometimes, venting stress but peace in time to find.
I don't think the trees listen or really pay attention,
but neither do they talk back and give me any dissention.
It's for these reasons and many more,
it's to these woods with all these wonderful trees,
I come here as often as I can my thoughts and ideas to explore.
To reach a state of serenity, to clear my mind, and think what I please.
Among the trees in that welcomed solitude,
I can address my problems and adjust my attitude.
When you're among such beauty it's hard to have an ugly thought.
Some calming meditation to sooth my soul as I settle into my green grassy spot.
If I'm not there physically, I often go there in my mind and I can see,
me among the trees with pen and pad in hand, writing more poetry.

Poem No. 54
As Long as I have Shelter

A source of heat when winter's winds are cold,
a roof over my head to keep out the rain,
as long as I have shelter, I can keep a hold.
  With very little, I could manage to maintain,
  my sanity, and my life regardless of what might unfold.

Having ample nourishment to physically sustain,
being capable of enduring the challenges yet untold.
  There is still another kind of shelter to seek and retain,
  emotional shelter for your mind is a treasure to behold.

In my quest to live my life, as I have become old,
there were times when no kind of shelter I could sustain.
  In my darkest hours, against so many forces uncontrolled,
  I longed for some shelter in a stormy life to shield me from its pain.

A physical structure can protect you from the elements, over and over
again,
survival assured, security and peace of mind against whatever can't be
foretold.
  Emotional shelter much more elusive, much rarer, and harder to
obtain,
  A true love can be such a shelter,
  if found, hold on to it tighter,
  it's more precious than gold.

The power of love is a very strong emotion,
supplying us sometimes with the necessary motivation,
the energy to rise above the worst of any situation.
  For me, there is no treasure more precious to gain,
  for as long as I have that shelter of true love, I can maintain.

Poem No. 55
Hanging Out with Doctors

I don't get out that much,
…these days.
Some say I'm way out of touch,
…in so many ways.
I don't really socialize,
…I never really did.
There is no church I patronize,
…I haven't since I was a kid.
These days I have very few friends,
…many have met their bitter ends.
I no longer want to get out that much,
…going out to bars, mingling and such.
With face masks and social distancing,
…I'm content with just reminiscing.

That's all right though, I've got a brand-new troop,
…I'm hanging out with doctors from my medical group.
They're a real fun bunch, complete with M.A.'s, Techs, and one trainee,
…my goodness, they always seem so happy to see me.
Through multiple office visits I see them quite regularly
…once or twice last month, this month it was three.
I have a whole team of fine doctors for my care,
…if I need anything, they're always right there.
Most people have a primary care physician,
…but with my team, I'm in a much better position.
I have my main doctor for my overall medical conditions,
…and man, she has the best medical intuitions.
If it concerns my heart, I've got a top rate guy,
…he makes sure the ticker keeps ticking as time ticks on by.
From my dear heart runs many, many vessels of all kinds,
…my vascular surgeon keeps a keen eye out there for dangerous finds.

(continued on next page)

My arteries and veins aren't what they use to be,
…she keeps them running clean and healthy.
She fixed my legs that were crapping out on me,
…even made my aching feet very happy.
There's another doctor who helps me deal with my back pain,
…He was first to help me regain the ability,
…to stand and walk again.
Yes, these days I mostly hang out with doctors,
…thank goodness, they're all first rate.
Each and every one of them is great,
…they should be in a hospital T.V. show,
…with their names up in lights so everyone would know.
Every one of them would be a star,
…but then, in my book they already are!

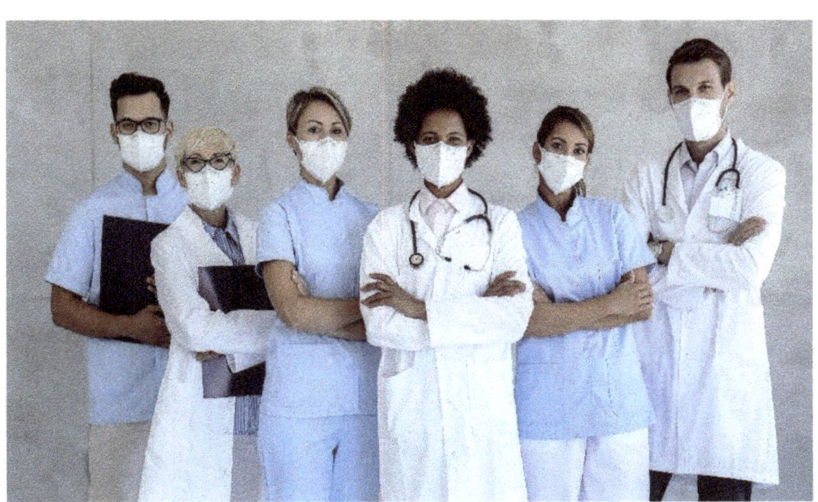

Poem No. 56
Pills to Go

At my local pharmacy,
I drive up to the drive-up window,
and I get my pills to go.

Now that I'm old don't you know,
I need a number of pills,
and the number continues to grow.

I've got pink pills that help make me go, (you know)
there are some yellow ones that I take,
so I can have some get up and go-go.

I have some red pills that help my blood flow,
more pills for an extra treat,
to keep my heart from beating too slow.

Twice a day, to make sure that all is okay,
I take two tablets with water to hopefully swallow,
purple in color, they keep my blood pressure low.

Then that's not quite all,
I have tiny little white pills,
I have to take them to lower my cholesterol.

There are pills I have for emergencies,
for when I can't go (you know), at all.
Every day I take pills to keep me alert and on the ball.

(continued on next page)

Four times a day there's my pills for my aches and pains,
extra strength pills, for when my body hurts from the strains.
Especially on those days it gets all cloudy, and it rains.

With all my pills to keep me alive and on the go every day,
I wish there was a better way, and I just wish there could come a day,
that I didn't need my "pills to go", and they could just go away.

Poem No. 57

There's Always a Body Count

Somewhere there's an old gray-haired man sitting in a large expensive leather chair,
(He has all his puppeteers there.)
In a prestigious office that is neither round nor square.
  He rules the East, and he rules the West.
  (he's only doing what he thinks is best)
The North and the South is at his command.
(He's the elected, the "selected", Leader of the Land.)
  With policies proposed and certain agendas set,
(Wait and see what the people will really get!)
  He's a large on a hill, white mansion resident,
  (They address him now as Mr. President.)
  Wielding all the power he needs to be relevant.
Decrees and laws are signed,
with the masses left resigned,
deceitful and devious plans are designed.
  Foreign affairs, new agreements and treaties start to flow,
  (Who and how will they benefit… no one will ever know.)
  while hidden offshore bank accounts burgeon as they grow.
With the economy on a big turn down it'll be a real tight season,
 dollars can't be spent without a good reason.
There must be something big, perhaps on a global scale,
a plan with enough funding that it cannot fail.
  The boys in the backroom will devise a strategy.
  an assassination done with care,
  maybe a small war somewhere, no one cares if it's right or if it's fair.
All their options are costly, but Mr. President and his gang will find a way.
  Money is really no object, they can always print more, tomorrow, if not today.
Many young men will have to fight, that cost is in lives, as many will certainly die.

(continued on next page)

While believing they were doing what was right, as the casualties continue to mount.
The Leader of the Land's carefully written speech said, oh well, it was our duty to try,
(Don't be naïve.) (This they say you must believe.)
it couldn't be helped, sometimes you just have to kiss it good-bye...
because you know... there's always a body count.
So, somebody had to fry.

A dictator of some country sits behind an oversized desk in some oversized chair,
his word is law, a heartless, soul-less man that rules by fear.
People do as they are told,
with no rights and any other options to hold.
  While the tyrants' greed runs hot and the blood runs cold,
  actions bold, a plan is devised that will be beyond grand.
A neighboring country, larger and much richer, there must be an acquisition of this land.
  For the power and the glory and the sake of someone's name,
  (God if it didn't happen, it would be a shame.)
The forecast is the battles will be fierce and the war will be long,
casualties taken will be high and as the obstacles surmount,
conscription of young men marching off to die for all the reasons that are wrong.
(Don't you know, there is no choice, you must go along.)
Never mind the numbers on the board...there's always a body count.
Now there's nothing to see here, everyone move along.

In a small country an old white-haired man sits on a throne that they don't call a throne.
  Guardian and Ruler of some sacred word,
  making sure to everyone only one meaning is heard,
  he has the vision and a personal connection to the Deity, he, and he alone.
His dreams can become reality should he want them to be,
he dreamt of one world united under his conformity.

(continued on next page)

Whether actually being guided by a Supernatural Cosmic Force or not,
  all rules and laws of humanity were cast aside and quickly forgot.
Members of the congregation must go out throughout the world and
"teach" the "Way".
  An army we will send with you to fight the heathens in the jungles
where they stay,
  in case they don't want to listen to what you have to say.
  (That's where and when that Force comes into play.)
Let them resist and cling to their old ways all they want,
if we can't convert them,
we'll insert them…
(in the ground),
then we'll deal with the rest that's left around.
  Someone will have to do a head count,
  never mind the dead bodies…
  but you should know, there's always a body count.
You must always count the casualties.

The majority of the population, the masses repeatedly do ordain,
choosing one individual or group to ruthlessly reign.
(Or they allow it to happen and happen again and again!)
  Blindly and obediently, they follow like sheep to slaughter, like they
have no brain.
Dress it up, make it look so pretty,
package it just right and name it something real snappy.
  At the core, it's still called "control", and some seek to wield it totally.
Like a thief in the night, night after night after many nights,
Just a little each time they come and steal away each individual's rights.
  So many times, the ones in charge are there for their own aspirations.
The power, the fame, and most of all the money. [the CASH man!]
(If you think that they think about anything else, you're being real funny)
By lies and deceit on a very grand scale,
with the aid of the great presses that will touch almost everyone.

  Their plans will be insured, being carefully engineered not to fail,
  they won't be satisfied until they have it all, when all is said and done.

(continued on next page)

Filled with ambition and a drive that will not quit,
they'll continue to get after it.
   They'll say let some be protesters and protest,
    that won't bother them none,
    (No one can shoot you if no one has a gun!)
    If the resistance gets too loud …they're not too proud
    if the resistors should continue to resist,
    they won't care, they'll just call out their army should it persist.
(Mow them all down with their Mattel machine guns!)
Sometimes, some people have to die.
   Mostly there's no one that will ask why.
   (If they get in the way…they'll find a way, to explain it all away.)
It is so sad the way the world turns, and the wicked keep sliding on by.
   When money makes the "civilized" world go round,
   the lust for power and control with no compassion to be found,
   with false promises of greater freedoms, a more equal life they always
expound.

Life should be fairer …but it's never there
You must know the truth…they don't, and they won't ever care.
   Those with the gold make the rules they say,
    rules made for them to always win the games that they play.
Some will open their eyes and minds from time to time.
   Some of us see it all for what it really is, we know it's wrong,
   we've seen it's not fair, it's not right, it's evil and what's more it's a
crime,
   and we've known it for so long.
As always, we sit back and watch like we're just watching a movie,
hoping to ourselves like Hell that it won't come along and touch "me".
   While it still goes on and on,
    today is almost the past, tomorrow will be here and gone.
Things won't get better, they'll get worse,
as I see so many always put themselves first.
   Not until more people open their minds and hearts to see,
    behind the scenes there's forces trying to imprison all humanity.
While there's millions oppressed,
the rich and powerful become more obsessed.

(continued on next page)

Somewhere in a sleek shining office floating among the clouds high in the sky,
sits a very rich man, a very powerful man, he contemplates the next acquisition he wants to buy.
As he counts his account with his accountants he hired to count,
(Businesses, companies, officials and politicians, hell, countries if he should want!)
regardless the decision's consequences or collateral damage, profit is always paramount.
I've figured it out, the billionaires want to become trillionaires,
with anyone standing in their way must be taken out. For whom really cares?
Their one solution, a global economic coalition they've agreed is tantamount.
Suffering by many will be great, but not their concern, they will suffer not,
The elite and their own are never the ones that hurt as the hard times surmount.
Remember, there's money to be made in some war somewhere, it should never be forgot.
Someone has to pay the price, there's always a price to be paid,
over 50,000 dead, but there was over 100 billion dollars made.

While all the while we go about our lives, some of us, our blessings to recount,
we're so oblivious, but still deep down knowing, there's always bodies to count.
… and still, we continue to look the other way,
preferring not to know the whole account.
Isn't ignorance bliss, isn't that what they say?
Who really wants to know anyway,
how many died needlessly today… that died anyway?
It seems ignorant is how so many have chosen to stay.

(…and the dead and mangled bodies they continue to count,
their poor faces have been blurred.
By the hour they continue to mount,
… but maybe no one in the world, has heard, a word!)

Publication History of William E. David

Poems published by Underwood Press publisher of 6 online journals:

"A Dead Horse Fantasy", "Words Without Meaning", Sorry, But It's Not a Good Fit" published in the journal Underwood. "Belle's Saloon" published in the journal True Chili. "On Hold", "Among the Trees", "Freestyle", I Never Judge", "Early Morning Sunlight", "40 acres", "Dandelion Wine", Lunatics on the Loose", and "Pills to Go" published in the journal Rue Scribe

Poems published in the online journal, Elevation Review:

"Autumn Leaves" and "A Cloudy Day"

Poems published in the online and printed journal, Bluing the Blade:

"Re-boot #2"

Poems published in the online and printed journal, Sheepshead Review:

"Breathtaking" and "Waterfall"

Poems published in the online journal, Street Lit:

"Down on the Riverbank"

Poems published in print anthologies by Poets Choice:

"Monsoons Over Arizona" in the printed anthology, "Monsoons"

"Pushbuttons, Remembered" and "Walking on Ice, Recalled" in the printed anthology "You are Nostalgic"

"My Dog's Best Friend" and "Funny Little Guy", published in the printed anthology "Dedicated to Pets"

"Make an Adjustment", published in the anthology "Letting Go and Moving On" by Poets Choice.

Poems published in print anthologies by Wingless Dreamer Publishing:

"Inspiration at an Exterior Coastal Scene" published in the printed anthology, "Flee to Spring".

"The Best Years" published in the printed anthology, "Breath of Love",

"A Mountain Paradise, Outside of Seattle", published in the printed anthology, "My City line".

"Evil; Invisible Enemy", published in the printed anthology, "Field of Black Roses".

"Bubbles", published in the printed anthology, "Vanish in Poetry".

"Watching the Waves Wash In", "published in the printed anthology "Summer Fireflies".

"The Cosmic Machine", published in the printed anthology "Evening, Wine, and Poetry".

"Where I Come From", published in the printed anthology "My Sanskriti in teal".

"The State of In-between", published in the printed anthology "Unveil the Memories".

"Hard Times", published in the printed anthology "Cradle of Balladry".

"Snow in the Catalina Mountains", published in the printed anthology "Crystalline Whispers".

"Bird in My Tree", published in the printed anthology "Wings of Wonder".

"Waiting for a Train", published in the printed anthology, "Dulce Poetica".

"To Ease the Pain", published in the printed anthology "Growth in Grief".

"It's Water Under the Bridge", published in the printed anthology "Poetry on Life".

"We're Holding On", published in the printed anthology "Rhapsodies of Rhyme".

"Live Life While You're Still Living", published in the anthology "The Power of Hope".

"With a Slight Chance of Rain", published in the anthology "Whispers of Spring".

"Desert Wildflowers", published in the anthology "Wild Heart".

A Captive Heart" published in the anthology "Verses from the Rainbow".

"Super Moon over Dragoon" published in the anthology "The Surfi under the Mystical Moon".

"Peaceful Valley" published in the anthology "Whispers of the World".

"Carbon Catastrophe?" published in an open theme anthology by Wingless Dreamer Publishing. Title to be determined.